Bahman Amidi

The Yellow Dog,
the Never war
the Sudden War
And Death

Outskirts Press, Inc.
Denver, Colorado

Dedicated to:

Everyone who helped with the

experience both tragic and good…

The king and the battles…

To love and humiliation,

And to: Bob Dylan.

Contents

The Yellow Dog

It's getting blur...wake...

It's never too dark… wake…

For if it is too late…

You will remain asleep.

Inside my mind there is pain,

As an orange inside its peals...

I cocoon, in the doldrums,

Rumbled,

Beloved, desires living,

Tantalizingly,

Demoralizing, I sing,

Numb in terrify.

My mind's a diarchy,

No woe, in guarding.

Meaning cedes in breath,

And beloved is desired, romantically!

Follows mad divinity of familiar passion,

Grasps the wheels of decision,

At the peak of desire,

I say the word love, and go the choir:

Its fake white, is fake dark,

I stuck in her double (devil) eyes,

She strike with her soring smile.

Now many years pass and I'm alone,

Thinking wisely in a throne...

Thinking in secrets...

So truth reflects...

Shielding my home by sword!

The people of my town are dirty,

They blame the king for thinking,

But in faith,

There is one with everything,

There are some with some things,

There are many with nothing,

They are ones with not even nothing!

They blame the king for thinking.

I want to tell them to:

Stop eating,

But they won't and that's why,

They aren't as worthy as the queen.

The prophet cleverly invested in me,

And I, worshiped, worshiped for better days,

I differed...in a day,

And learnt not new but old words.

I am now the tree in my dream,

I am now the man with too many feelings,

The prophet says,

I am "every" branch,

But like you I don't see my own image.

Tonight I will go to drink,

With lovely ladies, I will betray,

Those... that play my heart in role,

Those that I can't throw, my decent emotions at,

Cause I am not decent,

I will toll at them, straight, sharp (emotions.)

The breeze does not calm,

The sudden war began.

With a coup for being the next god:

I'm close to the throne, with soldiers at stead...

To them I said:

"I'm the ghost, needn't live,

This the heart needled,

That still is.

Upon it, treacherous of all,

Lures lay...

Here the mirror weapon,

To infinite debt,

Here the mirror ye have built:

To the known victorious,

The known, shall

Shatter with.

The heavens will spoil,

And wrecked ships such may peace with sin."

God orders men in draught, to spread.

Vowing, Ridiculing, torturing their friends.

He was known of my intent.

O God, before you kill me,

Let me enjoy the last moments of life.

Six years have passed,

And I have not had sex,

My therapist says: I'm emotionless.

Women seem more beautiful than ever,

I'm not a virgin and I have kissed,

All in all I guess I'm cleverer,

Women pass and they smile at me,

That probably means I'm not bad looking.

It's like fate has a surprise for me,

Six years ago I fell in love,

Her eyes were green and her skin was white,

When I told her about it,

I knew what she would,

Reply,

She didn't feel as I.

There was pain and happiness in my heart,

Not only did I see her enough,

We often had fun, and hung out...

She was my first and maybe last,

And I was only fifteen.

Six years have passed,

Since I had sex,

My doctor says: I'm emotionless.

I met my imaginary friend,

Through a friend,

He is black and he is blond,

We often meet at sunny places,

And talk of our day,

I meet him now and then through dreams,

At café's and destroyed mental hospitals,

He is very against the government,

And yet he is a friend of them,

I want the old days back.

I'm in the English classroom,

Me: Can't you see you're nothing? You barely exist.

"Cheers."

Can this guy, read my mind?

"Yes, page sixty six."

Can she read my mind…

"What an idiot." Her eyes seem to say.

"So, man, what type of music do you like?"

Me: everything…I guess, you?

"placebo…"

Never heard of them…

"Yeah placebo. They're olrite."

"Page seven, Frau Brechenmacher, Mary, would you like to read?"

I can't follow anymore…

"Frau Brechenmacher did not think it funny…"

It was funny for him to stand and see,

As if it was a stupid fantasy!

His meetings would challenge constantly,

To vex him, blindfolded.

Long live their presence…

That lesson, sense, scent of his essence...

In me… there is a man,

Dark in and inside the dark,

With shades that will lift you about,

The world doesn't end, the stars will die…

As I, watched the stars… that night...

My friends were curious behind my back,

As I got up from my spot,

There she was,

Building her moments,

I came to say hello; to kiss your cheek,

Whence you kissed my lips and rewrote history,

I awakened from my sleep.

Love is your description,

And the rest escape.

Her hair shines,

I've never seen anything shine,

Her eyes look towards me,

And she smiles…

That mind that is nothing alike (mine,)

You are young and I am old,

Both grown to be read,

She is light red,

She cried a smile as I'm naked,

She's too perfect to be created.

She's not in love… the lover is satisfied,

But at times the lover is wanting,

And she smiles…

Now regretted of one another,

Every day… of our first meeting further,

So the jokes we make of us that are sharper than a knife,

But I will recall the key to your heart,

I will set myself free with you,

Lay my head on your shoulders, I'm a man,

Lay my head on your shoulders, I'm undead.

Even though time wanted to brutally make friends,

Even though I am a man,

My head on your shoulders, your head on my chest...

That I have faith in...

I am worshiping again...

I have faith in that...

That isn't God... isn't that.

That was born from a mother that named that...

That is that...and was given that...

God challenged that...

And claimed ruling for himself,

That rules none the less...

Whatever god steals...makes more intellect of that...

For god claims to be that...

That is a theory which priests stole... to fit their books of angels with this...

They yelled this is an angel...this is the prophet...

Calmly spoke that...is an angel and that is a prophet...

That is a word which you speak and see shapes of straight lines and math...

That is a saviour from all of the innocent murder of nature...

Say a prayer in that and you will know that...

True love is weak compared to that...Because that wanted to be like that...

I wait for the day that comes back...

And rules this world with only bliss...

What I am trying to say is that if the world is wrong...

That will never be right...that is the sacrifice...that will cry...if tears fall...that is...gone...

The king's feared,

His spies betray him,

As one of them lives and the other dies,

Love's turning its back,

Luck turning black, lucking coming back,

Less more less...

Sire falls madly in love with death,

He leaves,

The wasted gesture of him will be missed...

Evil laugh's at the cotton wearer, as he almost falls from his jokes,

The wool wearer looks to the left and laugh's from the heart of nature…

The earth is heating the globe,

I need wings, to flee the war,

Cities will to poor the streets,

This house needs a same aged friend…

The world is my room.

It is a world of worst case scenario,

All banning's are but images.

It is a world of opportunity…

A world of surprise…

Pick your frown up and enjoy life.

And solely… it was…

A wrong and right,

And so…there is…

Right ways of wrong, and,

…wrongs in rights…

As we old enough in disguise,

We're not feared to recognition,

These wrongs are to feral,

To those too perfectly positioned...

It's the morning and I'm alone...

They are asleep...and it's the night,

Don't push and hold,

To This fall,

As I carry, black flowers to the red rain,

Lay your head on my anger...

While beloved smiles...

She Stays as King

La pluie éminente sur la rose,

My faith has vanished, all my hopes…

My love do not touch my heart,

My hands scored swift; and I am bruised.

And the lilies at silence mirror-light,

Piquant less, at their right,

But so the question remains,

Was I invincible or invisible?

Father Quit

A man with a baby passed,

Smiled at me and laughed…

Woman your sister had it bad,

Ask the heart, pass it off,

Knows this world murders-whore's…

Should the dead be silent again, far off silent,

Silence wins…

In that heart-sometimes,

A stone swims…

Forgery, fantasy, solo sins…

I have not only paid,

I have bought.

Width and the Harp

Snow's carbon lets him believe:

Beauty resists in such manners.

Away I slept; awake in drunken courts,

And the rule was:

You walk as if you have wings,

For it is cast that only God can judge Judas.

Hail! I come forth to descend my gripping plot!

Heavenly servant, pious judge,

Your magnitude has sold many souls, to the seed of earth...

Eyes to eccentric fields...

Kings with cloaks and heartful wives, yes, I share thy pain for my name is not Moses.

Freedom is breaking the strings and piecing them together.

Oh children, ye hath made the sun the shine,

Nothing is not easy to find; for everything is calling.

I'm not an Excuse

Love was never a virtue,

From the beginning your beauty was absolute,

Around the watchful eyes of those gods,

I received some sinless mercy.

Stranger, you changed my days,

Strange one, you are beautiful,

Your dark hair with its flair,

After love started to wear off my heart,

Why did you come back and set it free?

Some days I wished never been,

Time froze in lies and bad things happened,

So I created an imaginary cellar,

Where I told the lord I'd stay,

And wait till any realize, love's missing.

Stranger, you changed my days,

Strange one you are beautiful,

Your dark hair and its flair,

After love started to wear off,

The sea waved rapidly.

So I'm here no matter how many years,

I will stay till I find my favourite mind,

Whose rosy lips and smile,

Though not for mine,

Shall never be lucid to others,

Stranger, don't come back,

Strange one go fall in love...

This book should be read with eyes that do not only want to read what the writer has to say, but wasn't intended to fade...

Bahman Amidi

Lightning Source UK Ltd.
Milton Keynes UK
UKOW021629211111

182438UK00012B/62/P